HAPPY MOUNTAIN, BEAUTEOUS LAND
—

A Collection of Poems

Robert K. Wen

iUniverse books may be ordered through booksellers or by contacting:

iUniverse
1663 Liberty Drive
Bloomington, IN 47403
www.iuniverse.com
1-800-Authors (1-800-288-4677)

ISBN: 978-1-5320-1369-0 (sc)
ISBN: 978-1-5320-1370-6 (e)

Library of Congress Control Number: 2016921180

Print information available on the last page.

iUniverse rev. date: 01/11/2017

Contents

Part 1
Short Poems

Part 2
Poems of Medium Length

Part 3
Long Poems

Part 4
Chinese Poems

Also by Robert K. Wen

In English:
Love Across the Pacific, published by Writer's Showcase and presented
by *Writer's Digest*, an imprint of iUniverse.com. Inc., 2000
Leaves Upon the River, iUniverse, Inc., 2003
Dream of Spring and Autumn, iUniverse, 2006
Religion—One Man's Overview, iUniverse, 2010
Philosophy—One Man's Overview, iUniverse, 2014

In Chinese:
华美人生，上海文化出版社，Huameirensheng，Shanghai
Culture Publishing House, 2005
春秋缘情，AuthorHouse, 2008
(Chun Qiu Yuan Qing)

Preface

Around the age of forty, I started to tinker with poetry writing when I had the time away from my work as a professor of civil (structural) engineering and had the inspiration that hit me. Before I retired from my profession at sixty-five, obviously I could only do this sporadically. This irregularity actually increased after retirement because I was mainly writing in other genres, like novels.

In almost a half century of my poetry hobby, in spite of a low rate of production, I note I have accumulated a fair number of poems, and thought it might be worthwhile to assemble them into a small book. This is done chiefly to serve as a record for myself. I also hope it may interest some general readers who would share certain aspects of my outlook on life and/or personal experiences.

The great majority of the poems represent my personal feelings and musings at the time of writing, although a few were created for some of the novels I wrote, and several were composed to amuse relatives and friends. Included herein also are seven in Chinese. They all have their English counterparts.

The assemblage covers a range of topics including endeavors for a material basis of life (job), family (now three children, their spouses, and eight grandchildren), and, of course, spirituality. Poetry writing for me is a combination in varying proportions of relaxing, therapeutic, uplifting, and exacting, and an overall enjoyable, experience. Mostly the poems are of the free verse type with no set meter or rhyme scheme. They are relatively straightforward, expressing a mood or emotion, and involve fairly simple imagery and symbolism.

For convenience, I have grouped the English ones according to length of the poems into short, medium, and long. Generally, short ones would come about from experiences akin to epiphanies, and longer ones belong to the more reflective type. In the table of contents, four groups are listed in the order of short (S), medium (M), long (L), and Chinese (C). "Short," taken arbitrarily, means to be no more than fourteen lines; similarly, "long" means having at least four cantos. Within each group, they are presented in reverse chronology. Each poem will be denoted by the year it was first written, and if there is more than one in the year, an additional numeral tag is included. For those seven poems with both English and Chinese versions, for cross-referencing purposes, an additional designation of "C" is attached to the year tag for the English versions. For each Chinese poem, an end tag of S, M, or L will denote the group to which the corresponding English poem belongs. A few photos are included to accompany some of the poems in hopes of adding to the flavor of the book.

Acknowledgements

I would like to take this opportunity to express my appreciation to Patricia Wen, Robert Ullmann, and Stephanie Ullmann for their encouragement and helpful comments on the poems and to Judy Wen for her support of the project. My thanks are due to Joan Ho for her professional work on the covers and internal image insertions. Thanks are also due to iUniverse for the copyediting of the book.

Part 1
Short Poems

The Autumn Equinox

I wake up from a foggy dream.
Westerly rain pelts the window screen.
Twisting and turning snarl the blanket.
I fling it, rise, and return to the booklet.

A Cricket

In the dusk of an Indian summer day,
A cricket in the bush was singing gaily.
I said, "Enjoy it now, you little guy!"
"You too. You too," he muttered in reply.

S.2003.C

Recent Events

Two viruses erupt in the East, Near and Far,
To decimate the flesh in fire or SARS:
One mutates from the common cold;
The other dwells in self-righteous hearts.

S.1997

I Am a Hen

I am a hen, sitting on this egg,
For hours on end, days and weeks,
Through cold and heat.
Now the ice melts, and the roof leaks.

I am getting old with feathers soaked.
I need to check the egg soon.
Woe! Woe! It is hard.
All along have I been sitting on a stone?

Drops of sweat drip down on my beak.
Is this a peck, knock, or a click?
Hallelujah! Hallelujah!
I hear the peep of a chick.

S.1996

Martian Clod

So excited are they about the Martian clod
That hints there is life in space elsewhere.
All the time I have been aware
That God is more than their God.

Each from Each

Each from each, they part in a dragging pace,
Looking back and ahead after the last tryst.
A few more steps, likewise, minding respect and grace,
But always again ahead, until each vanishes in the mist.

Over the Weir

It has been a hard winter—
Snow, ice, and deep freeze.
Over the weir, the ice glistens pretty.
It asks the spring sun to free
Its molecules to travel down the creek.

The sun says: When I give you freedom,
You'd no longer glamorous be.
It pleads: Glitter is not what I desire,
Only the space of the wide sea.

S.1991.C

A Leather Coat[1]

Short of means precluded a fetching dress,
The lad hankered attention still.
    He hankered attention still.
In dad's silk jacket, he went to meet the lass.

Years of chalking gets him a leather coat.
The man forgets the wrinkles on his face.
    He forgets the wrinkles on his face.
Straining his tired back, he sashays so.

---

[1] One weekend, I went to Ann Arbor to meet friends for diem sum, wearing my new black jacket. A friend commented lightheartedly, "It makes you look so young!" I wrote this to amuse all.

S.1990

Another Round

The past round has added
A few white lines above,
And dark ones below, the eyes.
Still the gilding of the morning window stirs;
The moon-silhouetted treetops calms.

Dear friends, with the grace of God,
Let's have another go
With muted gusto.

S.1988

Winter Solstice

Dark trees stand voiceless.
Barren branches outstretch heavenward.
Hidden deep behind the frosty skies,
A fiery sun inches toward the spring equinox.

S.1984

To Patty and Bob[2]

It has miniature roses, pink and white;
Smiling daisies with arms opening wide;
And lavender orchids perching like a crown.

In green ferns, carnations burn in flame.
I see a velvet flower—I know not its name—
And daffodils heralding joyous spring.

Thank you for your thought on this evening.

---

[2] Daughter Patty and son-in-law Robert Ullmann sent flowers as congratulations on my Distinguished Faculty Award in 1984.

S.1983

Intellect[3]

Intellect will never grow old.
A warm body will someday be cold.
Intellect is fresh and sublime.
Gimme that body anytime!

---

[3] This is a joke with friends.

S.1980

An Egg Girl

By a Jiangsi[4] railroad track in a fall dusk,
A girl holds overhead a basin of a dozen eggs.
With gravel underfoot, wobblingly she moves,
Window to window, upward looking,
Hoping to have the eggs sold
For the pittance they would bring
When she should be inside a warm home
On such a chilly evening.

---

[4] This is a province in southeastern China.

S.1978

Seeing J. C. Ku[5] in San Francisco

Chance had it that we shared our youthful days.
We roamed the enchanting grounds like young bucks.
The land tremored; we went our sep'rate ways.
Mindful how little prepared I was, luck
Sent me off to learn what should have learned.
Then the half-witted student strove to teach,
While the real builder, after the shacks burned,
Build dwellings for a million near the beach.
Time fell like dust over ten thousand miles,
Decade of dust wiped off by a phone's ring.
Old banter failed to hide the joy; sweet smiles
Beamed on the young. Ah! The pride they bring!
Old friends are like old wine, yet can't be bought;
In them the lost years may again be sought.

---

[5] College classmate, roommate, and best man at my wedding.

14

All Shall Come to Pass

My philosopher friend told me:
"The gains and the losses,
The jubilation, the suffering,
The gathering, the parting,
The exultations, and humiliations,
All shall come to pass."

I thought about it and said to myself:
"It is because I know that
I shall and will always return to the home
That I am making the journey."

S.1977.2

A Distant Horn

I hear a distant horn.
This is your field.
Plow it.
Plow it.
I rise, rub my eyes, and take the hoe.

At the patch I strike.
Nothing gives.
Again and again,
Scratches and indents appear.

Again and again,
Fissures show like honeycombs
Again and again until it becomes soil fit to seed.

I lie down to rest and wait
For the distant horn to again call me
To work the soil for my feed.

My Job

I clothe, house, and eat,
But do not sew, build, or plow.
My students I teach.

Winter's End

Light snow covers the land.
Blue smoke winds up the sky.
Clouds slowly transfigure.
A man muses by the world's side.

A Stormy Night

The curtain lights up and is gone.
The heaven blasts open with a clap!
I wrap the blanket tight around.

The rain begins to hit the roof,
Like hordes of little horses on fast hoofs.
Drips drum the gutter; gush splashes the ground.

I bend my knees and wriggle my toes.
Waves of night wind come and go.

S.1972.2

A Pebble[6]

On the ground of the parking lot,
A pebble gleams in the fading sun.
I kick it and watch it skid and run.

Like a soccer player, I carried it
All the way to my waiting car.
I can't remember when I played with a pebble last.

---

[6] This poem followed my leaving the office one afternoon on a summer consulting job for Sargent and Lundy in Chicago.

Moonlight (A La Li Bai)

Moonlight blanches the room.
I lie abed alone.
I like to watch the moon
With my mind on my home.

S.1971.1

A Rabbit

In the quiet morning and between the flower beds
Squats a fluffy creature with a cottontail.
What a picture of peace and beauty
That evokes our reverence and piety!

If there are many more of its kind,
We'd be with clubs in hand and violence in mind,
Chasing the critters and crushing their heads
That can't time to be pets or pests.

The Indulgence of the Tongue

Whether it's a yearning for recognition,
A gnawing at the cocoon of loneliness,
Or a pathological escalation of amiability
To impress, flatter for gain, or work to persuade,
Like hamsters addicted to their wheels,
The lip and tongue weave in perpetual motion,
Spinning out a web of words senseless,
Trapping the speaker and the listeners alike.

Each word is a bit of respect lost,
But too late to check the lips' momentum.
The stomach tight and mind a desert, all owe to the tongue.

High School Football Banquet

The coach speaks on with increasing conviction,
"Football is an integral part of boys' education.
It is life, a creative art,
And great for character building.
A great bunch of guys!"

This fine runner and punter
Wouldn't complain about the pain
After being tackled out for the season.
Always giving a hundred and twenty percent,
He has not played since for that reason.

The player's little brother asks his mom,
"When are we going home?"

Before Boarding

The lad is going overseas.
Mother hands him gold rings, a pair.
In secret, the lass wipes off her tears.
Father reminds him to take care.

S.1967

To My Children on Christmas

Christmases come; Christmases go.
The year is passing. May you grow
Taller, stronger, and more handsome
And gain in knowledge and wisdom.

You'll be considerate and good
To each other and others too.
Learn to practice the Golden Rule.
You'll be happy every Yule.

Mother's arranged the Christmas tree
To fill our home with warmth and glee.
As my gift for the Nativity,
I give you this short poetry.

Arthur, Patricia, and Marco Wen (1967)

Part 2
Poems of Medium Length

M.2016

A Fall[7]

The fireplace ablaze,
Holiday tunes wafted in the air;
My cup runneth over; all sixteen of us will be here.
I was flying high, rushing after the lad
To the challenge of a ping-pong game.

A step missed between the rooms without a door,
Headfirst I dropped from the air like a shot duck,
Lying over the linoleum-covered concrete floor,
Awaiting the next page of fate or luck.

I am old; my body feels cold.
What was that cracking sound?
What is this warmth streaming down the cheek?

"Grandpa fell on the ground!"
The nine-year-old summoned his dad aloud.

In a generation turnaround, a gentle voice:
"Can you hear me? Don't move."

---

[7] This occurred January 2016 after an accident in winter holiday.

There was not enough life to move or speak,
Merely an existence weak.

Angels wheeled the body in and out
Of the chariot and the tube
And stitched over the eye an extra brow.
You will be good and careful now.

A year ago, he would've just stumbled and recovered.
I am old; my body feels cold.
It had been descending but didn't tell the mind.

Now I hear the landing gear groan and grind.
Would it be tidy if I did land under the floor?
No, no! Miles to go!
Miles to go?

All 16 of us (Christmas 2015); Left to right: First Row, seated:
Nathan, Olivia, Audrey, Robert, Judy, David, Michael;
Second Row, standing: Rachel, Vickie, Art, Suzanne,
Marco, Patty, Robert Ullmann, Katie, Stephanie.

M.2008

The Sichuan Earthquake, 2008[8]

I see the multi-story school with whitewashed walls.
I see the cheery, backpacking children on their bikes.
I see the apple-faced maidens fluttering in the dining hall.
I see the unshaven workmen bricking by the hillside.
I wish you all are safe and sound.
But what can I say to the thousands underground?

There is no need to tell of your sorrow and guilt,
Of having enjoyed the sights and leaving aglow
To write your hedonic lines with a lilt.
Would your modest donation lighten the blame?
Would it suffice to attend the candlelight service?

Or would you point your finger at heaven and declaim:
"Where were your love and your grace?
Should we now deny you our devotion and praise?"

What can you do to help the dead? To a rebirth?
You could talk of grief, faith, love, and compassion,
Besides accusing heaven and faulting the earth.
Better rewrite the check and triple the donation.

---

[8] This poem refers to the calamity in which 70,000 people died, occurring
    six months after a group of friends, my wife, and I had enjoyed a memorable
    tour of that very region. See "L.2007.C—An Enchanted Trip."

M.2004

A Dog

Snow renders the outside a fairyland.
Torn metallic wrappings, strewn on the floor,
Glint with tinsels, and colored lights twinkle on the spruce.
Most children and grown-ups have had theirs.

The mother says to the gentle boy, "Here's for you from us."
He opens the envelope and reads slow but loud,
"You promise to take care of it responsibly …
After you return from camp next summer …"

Up the boy throws his hands up with a wild yell, "A dog!"
He thrusts himself into the embrace of his mother sitting on the
    floor.
Hands clasping her body, head on her shoulder, silently they rock.
Getting up, he picks his way towards the father standing by the door.

Like a feisty schnauzer, he leaps onto his bosom and
Hugs the neck with his feet clasping the waist at the back.
Younger cousins goggle with open mouths.
Others smile, gladdened for the enraptured lad.

David Ullmann and Hudson

M.2003

Warm Sea in Winter[9]

The clanging reggae is not for me.
The psychedelic dresses and bare limbs are not for me.
The enormous mouse amuses me not,
Nor Snow White, Daffy Duck, or Pinocchio.
I don't want my puckered face on a photo,
Nor brown spots in side mirrors,
Nor angular legs on white sand.

I could go on imitating a grouchy poet
On this warm sea in winter.
The boat and everything of it are theirs—
The children and families of their own, all bright-eyed.
It's time to hand over the baton and step aside.

The waves roll, rise, climax, and break.
Bursting into piles of pearls, they recede and disintegrate.
The protean mass reforms and begins to roll again.

---

[9] I and Judy were on board *Disney Magic* with Arty, Vickie, Patty, Bob, Marco, and Suzanne, along with our grandchildren Stephanie, Katie, David, Rachel, Michael, Audrey, and Olivia in January 2003.

Born we are to be nurtured, to strive,
Smell the roses, drink the wine,
Smelt the soul from the body,
Take our turns to bear our own,
And continue and complete the destiny.

Youngsters put on ribbing skits[10] to entertain,
Not out of obligation but good cheers,
For a celebration of the shared blood in the veins,
And/or simply shared love in the heart.

And how many are blessed as honored guests
Sailing on this warm sea in their winter?

---

[10] This is at the expense of their grandparents, who allowed the production only because their parents paid for the expense of celebrating the grandparents' fiftieth wedding anniversary.

M.1998.1

The Magpies Calling[11]

With the magpies calling and wheeling above,
You come lithely like the Weavess,[12]
Down the celestial bridge arching across
The Pacific waves ten thousand miles wide
And two decades of a plodding life.

Jiang-nan's[13] scents are fresh and her voices gay.
Together we tame the flood of numbers stream.
Together we search the old country's days,
Past, passing, and to come for roots and dreams.
No more is the mute lamp my only mate.

---

[11] This is a love song in my novel, *Love across the Pacific.*

[12] Chinese mythology has it that, Weavess, who had lived east of the Milky Way, became derelict in her weaving after she married Cowherd and moved to the west of the Milky Way. The angered Heavenly Emperor ordered her back to the east and allowed the couple to meet only once a year on a bridge across the Milky Way, accompanied by magpies, on the seventh day of the seventh month.

[13] Jiang-nan means "south of the Yangzi River."

Dazed by the dazed eyes, I wander and wonder
In the musky valley and on saline peaks
And lose myself in the spiraling deeps.
Long fingers crochet a net upon my back,
As though I'd flee; my tongue tip is branded black.

O scintillations! O tenderness and passion!
How you lead me into the Fifth Dimension!
A vibrant existence, ineffable sensations
Nonexistent in the workaday domain!
Without them a bland life would remain.

I'll seal them in these lines as deposition
When summoned to sessions of silent thought
And pray for your care and benediction.
I'll go do my share; nothing else need be sought,
For I have known the Fifth Dimension.

Spring

Like an office worker fearing weekend's passing soon,
I would regret a too-early bloom.
But the cool air has prolonged the precious state
Since the colors emerged from last year's grave.

Mayapples under green canopies pray.
Tulips and daffodils sway in the wind.
Wild geraniums hail graceful trilliums,
And lilies of the valley their sweet bells ring.

Trunks sheen like metal polished,
Casting shadows straighter than them,
Like some heroes' fame. Sprays shimmy and wave,
Like excited hands in the Stock Exchange cave.

Bright blue jays land, hop step, and flap away.
Treetop cardinals in rising whistles duel.
Strutting crows jarringly cackle, and squirrels
Chase one another in a mad scramble.

The girl next door above the trampoline tumbles,
Aglow with the glowing redbud tree,
As her dad grimly pushes a cart of grass feed
And the barking dog strains the leash in its leap.

Stow these sights and sounds well.
Passing three quick summer months of fun,
November westerly rains blow the trees barren.
As you bend to lift the wet snow and grunt
To pry the truck-left ice mess by the driveway,
Retrieve the present sights and sounds to look ahead.

M.1993.C

Happy Mountain and Beauteous Land[14]

For millions of years, the mighty plates thrust
To raise the thick granite from the earth crust.
The valley walls the glaciers patiently ground.
Snow-fed streams made soil of the ground.

The sun and moon alternate; lives proliferate.
To the sky the redwoods rise straight, and
The Grizzly Giant by seven centuries Christ predates.
Here are the Happy Mountain and Beauteous Land.

Quivering sequins glitter in blue heaven.
Yellow lights hang from cabin eaves by the gravel road.
The heated air purrs; the family talk abed low.
The night wanes, winds calm, and eyes begin to close.

---

[14] In October 1993, our son Arthur invited his mother and me for a
vacation at Yosemite. After three days, tired but gratified, I wrote the
lines. "Yosemite" sounds like "Yue Shan Mei Di." In Chinese, it could
be 悦山美地, which means "Happy Mountain and Beauteous Land."
The Chinese version of this poem appears in part 4 of this booklet,
C.1993.M.

On the cliff, lodge specks of pines centuries old.
Tree roots snare boulders like boxers in a hold.
The coyotes howl, stirring the grazing deer.
Hanging silver streams plunge through rainbow tiers.

Ascending gingerly, the son holds his mother's hand.
The father, panting with a camera in tow,
Wonders what good deed has he done that
Has him land on this Happy Mountain and Beauteous Land.

Art, Judy, and Robert in front of the Grizzly
Giant Sequoia (25 feet wide)

M.1991

An Early Spring

I hear the cardinal calling this forenoon.
The last year's leaves shiver on oaks high
Above winter twigs and green blotches strewn
Over the yard with puddles of melted ice.

The siege is nigh over. There will come
Daffodils, forsythia, magnolia, and cherry blossom,
Along with robins hopping, woodpecker knocking,
Red Cedar River bubbling, and ducklings wiggling.

In the sweet easy thoughts loom
The dissertation and journals on one desk,
Research proposals to read and referee on the other,
The earnest eyes from down the classroom,
And the gesticulations at the committee retreat.[15]
The mass troubles my mind.

I enter the heart's sanctum for a values-review
To array the mass of items in time and timing
For their serene execution or disposal.
What one sows in spring, with summer steadiness,
One reaps in the fall.

---

[15] A university committee on graduate studies and research.

M.1990

The Waves

The wave is charging,
Vanguard of wild spirits with white flying mane,
Riding a curving steel blue front,
Clashing loud on the rocks,
Roiling up there and trying for the clouds,
Whirling and beckoning the following swells,
Charging after roaring charge,
Ever growing, dipping low, and
Rising high.

For Thine is the kingdom
And power and glory!

The pounding abates; the impinging relents
Into swirling, foaming, and dripping
About the crag. The fury is spent.
The clouds dissipate.

The moon makes her slow appearance.
The gleaming trickles, kissing the rocks,
And quivers in diminishing sighs.
And there is peace.

Blessed are the meek,
For they will inherit the earth.

M.1986

A New Year

The dust cloud drifted, turned, and spiraled fast.
In flashing lights, the stars circle serene at last.
The fireball warmed the ocean.
Grunting monsters rising from swamps slouched past.
Howling apes climbed down the trees to talk
And sail the seas, and now in space they walk.

Champagne, tinsels, sequins, and airs
Are all but annual affairs.
Sweaty palms, sullen stomach, and smiles sweet
Pay for the daily animal feed.

The bones of acquaintances old
Lie under fields damp and cold.
So behind the cliff you go, like the gull
With buffeted wings, tired, aged, and dull.

This wintry night is no time to complain
Of fulfillment, loss, or gain.
Now a bit player writes not the script.
Neither thought nor plan changes a word of the writ.
So say your daily prayer and live your lot.
Who at this stage ever knows it?

A traveler, with a stamped ticket in hand,
The eyes blurring over the shimmering band
Of withdrawing shore lights of Auld Lang Syne,
Squints for a moment of tenderness. O Hark!
The distant morning horn awakens the heart
To resume its stout beat
Of yesteryears to drive the blood to stream,
Robust in every vein, in cold hour and heat,
To stay the course onward.
Enjoy the journey, and never retreat.

M.1983

Duck and Drake[16]

I heard laughter in the spring air
And the patter of little tennis shoes.
I saw flowing, wind-blown hair,
Craned heads, and dangling toes.

I was launched into a flight,
Greeting clouds and dragonflies.
I skipped and pirouetted,
Ahead of the expanding rings.

I am sinking—
The opaque,
The hoary, and the dusk
Into the dark slime and mud.

In darkness I shall dwell
Like forever
Until the next big crunch
And the explosion.
Then there will be laughter
Of freedom in the air.

---

[16] A children's play where a small, flat stone is thrown to bounce and skip
on a water surface.

A Summer Evening in Pleasanton[17]

1

The golden tapestry dims behind the hillside.
Stars emerge above the valley.
Distant barking ripples over this sea of quietude.
On the pasture, a lone oak ages one more day,
As dusk falls unawares into the night,
Yearning for the yonder window light.

The hills exhale the night breeze.
Brass chimes and white pines in duet sing.
Scented air brings flashes of faces in,
Like little fish gliding in and out
Of a coral reef niche.

Each face is a remembrance, a tune,
A mist, and a silent sigh
Or a light glow, smile, and good-bye.

---

[17] This was written during the summer of 1978 when I worked for Lawrence Livermore Laboratory. I lived alone until wife Judy and son Marco came later.

2

These hills and valleys will surely outlast
Constructs of computers and nuclear technology,
Oleander-lined highways and rose gardens,
Watered by rains ordained for other lands.
In time, these hills and valleys will likewise
Be mere molecules in a gassy whirl.

Be this the truth as well.
I am here and now,
In body and in spirit,
Singing my song for this blessed valley,
Serene like a starlit bay,
Harboring a decent people at their rest,
In glimmering lights their boats safely moored.
In these lines I'll keep this evening evermore.

M.1973

A Meeting of Scholars

Droning of the plane engine,
Droning of the room ventilation,
Droning of the long corridor,
Droning of the conference hall.

The speaker hams it up;
The discussers aim to impress.
Aspirants congregate 'round the near stars;
The near stars around the star.

The green grant exec a few easy days presumed;
Now asks his friend's leave to hide in his room--
A scared fox scrambling for a burrow
To escape from the persistent grant hounds.

Aged men loiter in the lobby.
The young gather to plan for action.
I walk back to my room to concentrate,
To sharpen up my lecture to keep my class awake.

M.1972

Like a Kite

Like a kite, I fly high, and I fly low,
Looking over the pretty world below,
Riding the currents and waving in the air.
I thought on my own "I did them all."

For the string on me hangs loose.
It tugs only at moments of stall,
When I may begin to twist and fall,
Tearing my skin and breaking my bones.

I would soon forget the holder of my string
Sets the length and height I can go.
At times, I look at the blue heaven yonder
And am tempted to be thither by plunging into a gale.

Then I'd fear the string would in tension snap
And find myself impaled on a tree branch
Or an arm of some utility pole
Instead of reaching my fancied goal.

I can't forever be up here afloat.
I wonder when my holder would pull me
Back into his serene fold
Before the sun and rain rot me.

M.1971.1

A Hospital Room

She sits by the bedside, head bowed low.
The picnics and parties flash past the mind,
Like the color bands, through the venetian blind,
Cast by the lights of traffic down below.

Her world is cut into cool polygons
Of hallway lights on the ceiling and walls.
On them shadows of well-wishing plants
Quiver in the ventilation drone.

His eyes are closed; his color like wax.
Outside and down the hallway,
A robotic voice calls "Doctor X, Doctor X."
When could I regain a worry-free day?

Her mind dims into a blankness,
Blank like the black hanging TV screen;
Suddenly appears her hope and promise,
"After he recovers, every day I'll recall this scene."

M.1971.2

To the Shop

The golden bird lilts on a swaying bough.
Atop a cedar muses the wise owl,
Watching the sparrows hop about,
Pecking a grain or two.

Suddenly screeching cries rive the air.
The crows have arrived,
Darting wildly to and fro.
"Go! Go! Let's go!"

Into the woods withdraws the golden bird.
The owl opens his wings
And departs without a word.

I must go to the shop now
To build the contraptions
To quiet the crows' howl,
To push the boulders up and down
The dusty mountain route.

But it wouldn't be long; I'll return
To find the golden bird to hear it sing
Songs of beauty and eternal spring.
I'll seek out the owl
To look into its reflective eyes.
Is that a squinting-eyed sparrow-crow
Or a copper-sparrow writhing in academic fire?

M.1971.3

A Gap

I worked through depression, recession,
And hot, cold, and declared wars.
Silver threads, a charred pit, and curved back,
I gave 'em advantages myself never had.
They've become bold and cold,
Gone their own ways as they fledged.
They'd roam beaches and highways,
Flaunting their bodies and flouting decorum,
Pursuing no profession or trade,
En route to becoming bums or scums.
Sluggards and strangers oceans away
Freely get their solicitudes they'd withhold
From those who have sown their flesh and blood.

Why can't they understand?
They are setting examples for children of their own.
Why can't I understand?
I was young once.
Have I perhaps let my heart and mind too
Grow old?

They begot me out of lust,
Pampering me with all things but trust,
Claiming wisdom and viewing life only
Through the square tunnel their turbid times have dug.

The weary shadows stumble on:
Briefs, memos, plastic smiles,
Punched cards, conveyer belts, sweating hands,
Growth charts, Dow Jones, and cardiograms,
All are numb to the joy
Of righting blatant wrongs,
The iridescent sound, the sweet grass scent,
The wave-fondled feet, and sun-painted bust,
Hand-in-hand, at peace with land and sea
In calm or gust.

Why don't they ever learn from
The lessons of their parents?
I wonder, "Have they really known life?"
Maybe I'll find out
In time, unless I
Die young.

Tell Me

Tell me.
The leaves are but mere shadows,
Shaking against the sky, growing dark.
The cardinal gets in a last song.
It is dark, pitch-black.
I only hear the rustling.

Tell me.
There are so much beauty and truth to be sought,
Duties to discharge—so little talent, resolve,
And time. And I am weak,
Hurt, tired, and growing lazy with age,
Yet unwilling to concede.

Tell me.
Let me be forgiving and forgiven.
Let me rest;
Rest in this total darkness,
And be reborn in the morrow
When the sun comes to the window.

M.1971.5

Don't Raise Me

Don't raise me with your praises,
For I'd fall, snap my back,
And live with permanent braces.

Don't commend me on what I do,
For I may buckle
Under the weight of ego.

I am a mere ham,
Acting with wetting hands,
Trying to do more than I can.

Know you not what I have to pay,
A crippling ulcer
And anxieties every day.

So don't say I can be great
Unless you wish me
An early grave.

M.1971.6

Spring

I did complain about your coming late.
Now you are here at last.
My heart lifts as I watch you create.
But must you get on so fast?

Crabapple and peach trees put on new sleeves.
Buds unwind for a glorious display.
Willows and elms hasten to spout leaves
To provide for animals and people shade.

In the far horizon, dark clouds dissipate.
A golden veil rolls on the green meadow.
Glass beads glisten on fresh-scented blades.
Above the newly opened window,
Busy robins chirp and build their nests
Where they lay their eggs and rest.

After the egg-begotten robins first fly
Through the shades of leaves, then fully grown,
The flowers have blossomed with petals blown.
And the whirling maple pods,
Like so many wounded butterflies,
Have fallen on the lonesome path.

What shall have I known
Besides knowing that you
Have come and will be gone soon?

M.1970.1

A Dream

I was lying on top of a hill.
The air was fresh, cool, and still.
The firmament overhead was like a vault,
Huge and of color cobalt.
The crystal constellations twinkled in silent chorus.

The firmament begins to slowly rotate,
Carrying with it gleaming stars.
The air stirs to an easy breeze.
Wavelets of music softly undulate.
The hill rises inch by inch.
The jewels come within my reach.
I touch some but take none.

I thought I was alone.
But there was no loneliness.
I turned my head.
Against the blue grass, two limpid eyes
Were looking into mine.

My Try at Poetry

As a boy long ago,
I marveled at the soccer played by a star pro.
I would try to imitate,
With blood running fast in my legs
On the playing field of the school,
His footwork and sidesteps.
I got my kicks but rarely a goal.

Now my blood no longer flows fast,
And I run with ballast on my feet.
As youth leaves the body, experience
Enlivens the mind and pen on the sheet.

In my confused groping for the art,
I often pause and wonder:
It may be a sin of the heart,
Mere pretension, or even fraud
To groan or moan when there is no pain
Or for things there is no need to explain.

Still this urge and pulse inside
Simmer and refuse to be denied.
Though my pen is slender and crude,
The ink still seeks to go through.

Under nature's starlit skies
In the sweet air of the night,
Amidst songs of nightingales,
Frogs have right to tell their tales.

Thanksgiving

My Maker! My shelter everywhere!
How can I thank Thee?
How can a bird thank the air?
How can a fish thank the sea?

Should gratitude a burden bring,
Like the pressure on a fish deep sea
Or like the current 'round a gliding wing?
This burden gladly I'll ne'er be free!

As a contented fish in water
Slowly tilts its silver fins,
Quietly I consider and wonder
My luck and my blessings.

As a late bird lighting in its kin's nest,
Utters a few chirps, light and subdued,
I lower my head to my chest.
My Maker! Accept my gratitude!

M.1970.4

A Side Trip[18]

It's a light sweetness mostly I taste in this state,
Half-asleep and half-awake, to loll and ruminate
A side trip yesterday to revisit a place
Where I used to work, study, and self-cultivate.

The old boss still possessed his natural grace
Offering help, if needed, from his base.
Watching people around him hard at work,
I knew he was still setting the pace.

Friends greeted me with hearty gestures.
We talked of the past, present, and future,
Enjoying friendship while the children play.
All agreed it's part of our daily nurture.

---

[18] This poem came after a side trip, when attending a conference at Lafayette, Indiana, to Urbana, Illinois, where I had studied and taught.

I returned to the dorm late at night.
Morning sun woke me up with its bright light.
Not only there is a meeting to attend,
The queasy stomach wants to munch a bite.

Besides, there's a progress report I need to amend.
As if these weren't enough to halt my pensive bent,
Sweeter thoughts stirred up.
I shall be home by day's end.

Waking Up by Bird Song

Little bird, why do you sing
Incessantly such haunting tunes that ring
Through the thick woods and o'er the blue lake
And to this August morning me awake?

Are you complaining 'bout your common lot?
The color of your plumes pleases you not?
Is it about a nicer nest or easier seeds
That you consider your basic needs?

None of these would explain your song.
The greedy breed you don't seem to belong.
Likely it's an old ode of thanks you sing
To heaven I've not noted 'til this morning.

More blessed than mere birds are; we would plot,
Aggress, and struggle for more than we've got.
For a soul, he'd get to where anxiety leads.
For nations, thousands die like mowed-down weeds.

Little bird, are you telling us something
Past reason worldly things we've been chasing?
It is not too late to apply the brake,
To change our ways and peace with ourselves make.

Here and beyond, little birds sing along
Over wide waters, deserts, and jungles by Mekong.[19]
The weary warriors might heed your song.
A truthful truce could yet come and stay long.

---

[19] A major river in Southeast Asia that enters the South China Sea through Vietnam.

Part 3
Long Poems

L.2007.C

An Enchanted Tour[20]

1

They say Sichuan roads are hard for the aged.
Go anyway, and be wild for a change!
With three thousand miles and the Pacific in between,
We come to the embroidered beds of Tibet Inn.
In a rocking bus, rocking songs we chorus;
At the guide's stops, songs of nature one could sing.[21]

Judy at entrance of Tibet Hotel, Chengdu.

---

[20] translated from the version in Chinese; see herein part 4, "C.2007(L): 西川行." The tour was enjoyed with a group of friends to Jiuzhaigou Valley (九寨沟), one of the most famous areas of natural beauty in China, inscribed by UNESCO as a World Heritage site.

[21] "To sing songs" is the tour guide's euphemism for "to use the restroom."

71

Tour group of friends.

A small heater keeps the night warm
'Til morning's trip to the Pearl Shoal,
Rapids and waterfalls, a heavenly scene.
A fairyland is the many-colored Jade Pool.
Night singers' tremolos[22] pluck guests' heartstrings.
To each guest, a gift of shawl perfects the evening.

2

By the Ming River Tablet[23] fourteen thousand meters above sea,
A shout of joy from the yak rider greets the sight.
Night rain falls like threads on Song Pan's cobbled street,[24]
As we go for the spicy Ma-po tofu with ground meat.

---

[22] Tibetan singers in a theater
[23] Marking the source of the major river in the region.
[24] Song Pan is an ancient walled city, a fort.

Robert on yak back.

3

In Wen Zhou's[25] Tea House, waiting for the road to clear,
They play Sichuan mahjong with rules queer.[26]
With tea of wolfberry and chrysanthemum,
The wise man explains the wisdom of Buddha
Until the road opens; in twilight
We arrive at Wo Long[27] to visit the pandas

4

In the midst of clicks and chatters, the animals,
Relaxed and nonchalant, lounged, ambled about,
Or just chew twigs of bamboo.
"You guys better keep your number low,
To maintain your being pampered so."

---

[25] Wen Zhou was the epicenter of the calamitous earthquake that occurred six months after our visit.

[26] Only "three of a kind" type of form (peng or 碰) is allowed to incorporate a discarded block.

[27] Site of China's Panda Research Institute.

A group of pandas at the Panda Research Institute.

Yu Zui[28] divides the Ming River into flows of two.
The two further branch to run in four.
The scheme fans out to water the fields of Chengdu
For millenniums to keep the rich crops grow.

5

In Jin Sha, the gold masks[29] challenge its sons.
They built a world-class museum in response.
In an open kitchen of Ya An, a hefty cleaver drops;
The head of a giant silver carp ends in the visitors' chops.

Over mountain folds surrounding Lo Ding,
Up and down, dozens of turns the bus makes.

---

[28] It is a man-made isle, part of the flood control and irrigation system known as Dujiangyan. Legend has it that the project was conceived and carried out around 2000 BC. It has been credited mainly to the legendary Emperor Yu (2200–2100 BC).

[29] Found in a site of ruins (discovered in 2001) of an ancient civilization.

There wait servers of Love Song Hotel of Kang Ding,
Descendants of Persian troops of Alexander the Great,
Who had roamed eastward and intermixed, they say.
On the handsome lads, the ladies' eyes tirelessly lay.

6

High above the waves of the Da Du River,[30]
The iron chains of the bridge shake and sway.
In the warm sun and brisk wind,
The tense ladies squint only straight ahead.

7

Amid twilight the bus pulls in
The lodges at Ming Zhu Compound, elegant and serene.
At dinner's end, the lights go out, and all early turn in.
Next morning the peaks glitter golden to say,
"Another blessed umbrella-free day."

The cable car surveys an ice world from on high.
Between snowy hill slopes, a blue glacier lies.
On the grounds of Camp Number Three,
Barley cakes dunked in a hot bowl of yak brew
Warm the body in the frigid breeze.

By the hot spring-fed pool above pool,
Visiting beauties twitter and hesitate.
The bare-chested hero shows up the camera.
The ladies start to ease into the warm water,
Smiling, bantering, and gay.

---

[30] A key battle site where the Nationalist government attempted, but failed, to halt the Long March of the Communists in 1935.

8

Past the Er Lang Tunnel four thousand meters long,
We pay respect to the giant Buddha in Le San.[31]
With a magnetic heated dinner done, it's time to set off for Er Mei.
In a four-star lodge, we cleanse the travel dusts away.

9

Up the Er Mei Mountain, the bus winds its way.
Buddhist chanting permeates the mist.
The Golden Buddha appears as the fog melts away.
Facing the downhill course of wet slabs of stone,
I'd rather pay a litter's fare
Rather than risk my ankle on a buddy's dare.

10

It has been a fortnight of carefree living,
No thought of assignment, project, or strife.
To Lansing returns the face sunburned, the eyes bright,
Back to the bustle of making a negotiating life.
Mind not the winter nights may seem long and dreary.
Close your eyes; the enchanted sights would reappear, dearie.

---

[31] The seventy-one-meter-tall statue was carved out of a cliff.

L.1982

Reminiscences of St. John's[32]

1

Daydream is not for one past half a century.
He ought to till his field and mind posterity.
Let the past be shut like a closed mine.
Surely lingering there is a weakness sign.
The weak survives not, sentiments despite.
Man lives to work; only work makes a life.
My copper sparrow[33] says no,
Flapping his wings and fussing in the cage to and fro.
Therefore I sit myself down and sing a song
To soothe the bird before the tilling may go on.

2

I hear the chimes and a call,
Rushing back years one and a half scores
And come under the cupola of S.Y. Hall.
By the balustrades I stand, holding
The Suzhou River-embraced grounds in my ken.
To the left, Mann Hall guards the bank,

---

[32] After a visit in 1980 to the defunct St. John's University campus in Shanghai since I left it in 1949, memories of the grounds haunted me to write the verse in 1982.

[33] See M.1971.2, "To the Shop."

Buttressed behind by the Engineering School,
Where Dean Young taught us to make our tools.

Behind the stone arch gate carved with adages,
Like a palace, the Social Hall rises
By the tree-lined walk curving to the main gate.
To the road's right, the wide meadow extends past
Where the majestic Camphor Tree presides.

Thither the Low Library waits in quietude,
And the pointed chapel roof forever prays.
In the steeple's shadow nestles a cozy pad
For Miss Brady,[34] where the choir serenaded.
Toward the arch gate, the green lawn rolls back
Like a carpet unfolding, past the Yen Hall colonnaded.

3

I hear the chimes for the midmorning break.
Behind the chapel side door, the custodian darts
To pump the organ as the service starts.
Reverend Baker is here to keep us straight.
Some have come to sing,
Others to meditate,
With David Peng bowing for the pleading Massenet.[35]
Elsewhere in threes or fours, they form
Upon the stone steps, around the sundial, the arcade,
To lounge or break for a stroll on the knoll,
Chatting, enjoying the company,
Or sitting under the camphor tree's bowl
To lilt a quartet of harmony.

---

[34] Choir conductor.
[35] Massenet's *Meditation*.

A quartet; Left to right: Robert Wen,
Frank Huang, David Peng, John Tai.

4

I hear the chimes. Soon it will be the due date;
The work on mechanical drawing may be late.
To ink a screw in three ways of fine lines,
Hidden or full, some curved and others straight.
Under the candle, I carp at a task so delicate
'Til a sizzling sound and charred smell
Frightens my roommates to yell,
"Hey, your hair is burning!"
Mechanical arts, I master not.
I learn to persist in trying.

A civil engineering student surveying team in Changshu, about a
hundred miles from Shanghai, in the summer of 1948; Left to right:
Cai Chong Yao, Wang Min Zhi, Qu Hong Shou, Jiang Da Hua,
He Shang Yuan, Guan Jin Qiu, Wen Guo Liang (Robert Wen).

5

I hear the chimes amid sounds of music,
Of pipes of flesh and silver and strings and bows,
Followed by debates on whether the coast or inland
Produced most of China's heroes
Or whether life began in the seas or land,
Or God has to do with the Theory of Evolution,
Or is there life elsewhere in the constellation?
All oblivious to a civil war in the nation.

The chimes come and go.
The forensic zeal wanes.
Prickles on the conscience grow.
Be it resolved to burn the midnight oil!

Desks are wiped; sleeves rolled,
Tea leaves waiting for the water to boil,
But warm beds win out over the will to toil.
Under the comforters the scholars slide.
Again topics drift; books unopened lay aside.

Ominous knocks on the door silence the chatter.
Enters the young supervisor proud and loud.
In stern tone and visage, he proclaims the order,
"The gabbing must stop, and candles be out!
Lest all offenders will surely flunk!"

Yet the honey tongues of his charge have more clout.
The surrender completes as he joins in the fun
And climbs up onto a vacant upper bunk.

Old college roommates in front of Michigan State
University Main Library (1989); Left to right: Robert
Wen, Thomas Zhu, Kenneth Ku, John Tai.

6

I hear the chimes,
As I saunter up the Suzhou River bank in the night.
Huddling in the shadow of the moonlit bridge,
Like migrating fowls, napping boats
Wobble on wavelets in sheens black and white.
Lights flicker in hedge-fronted faculty abodes,
Row by tidy row, ranging by the riverside.

Out of the physicist's window, notes of reed
Pop in the air and can't no more be found.
The professor is testing the theory of sound.
The theory pales against the strains of a song,
Like the overhead leaves swaying,
A maiden's pious voice softly telling.

I walk by the rose bush in the window light,
Careful not to tread on the flowers' shade
And touch the petals lightly, lest they break,
And lift my head in the river breeze.
I draw a rose-scented breath and resume my gait.

7

Around the president's house, the river bends,
Tracking upward into the Caucasian quarters I loop.
Inside the low-lit cottage, joyous Bach
Beats the phonograph of Dr. Throop.

In the offing, the hulking camphor tree looms.
The shadows of a couple glided past.
Into the darkness they are lost.
The Low Library is dark, the chapel without a soul,
Save the enameled saints above the dew-bossed ivy,
All silent in the portico's yellow lights,
Shimmering in a visitor's childlike eyes.

St. John's University Chapel at night, 1948.

8

Away from the paved walk, crossing the thicket,
Opens the High School soccer and softball field,
Where routinely I drop an easy fly ball
Within sight of the modernized Shu Jen Hall.
Past the sycamore-guarded Gymnasium
For ping-pong, basketball, and an icy pool,[36]
Ranges Seaman Hall, where behind its ogling eyes
Dumas' tales; Szema Chien's chronicles;
Sex lives of earthworms; lens with candles,
Inverted and upright; and theories of all kinds
Cast images and seeds onto fresh, young minds.

The night is deep.
Over the field, pale vapor patches creep.
The breeze sweeps them to the hollow,
Nudging the drooping dandelions in their sleep.

---

[36] Filled by well water.

On the masonry platform commanding the nightscape,
I lie down and palm the nape.
The great vault descends,
Enveloping the buildings, trees, field, and me.
Slowly it withdraws.
The buildings, trees, and field all recede.
The stars lightly ring; the platform and I rise,
Wafting up the deep blue sea.

9

For three decades, I had left the grounds.
Those scenes would on occasion return to tell the days
When a young man's heart came to know a child's happiness
Enjoyed in an adult's freedom and form,
But sans his responsibilities.

Alas, they came soon enough, and the years flowed past.
The dusts from cares and strifes would fall.
The body declines; the heart grows weary.
The reminiscences of dear friends, places, and unfelt changes,
Like a morning breeze, would lift from under the dusty layers,
Up the heart for a retrieval of and celebration of
That kind of life's beauty that is mine to keep
Until the day when decline shall turn to decay
And the soul merges with the Way.

10

Once again I came under the cupola of S. Y. Hall.
No chimes were heard, and no arch gate was in sight.
The downspouts lay crimped; the walls were perforated.
Elsewhere, cinder replaced grass; the chapel looked dilapidated.
Dingy boats crowded the river.
Weeds strewn the walk,

Leading to a dead end at the bend
Where chickens picked and dogs balked.
"Where is the beauty?" my sons asked.
Like my youth, it was displaced.
But a mason tries to build it a dwelling place.

11

The beautiful grounds were but an oasis.
Had you ventured then outside your paradise?
Did you notice only by a stone's throw from the gate
The filth by the sides of the alleys and streets?
And hear the pleadings and cries of disabled beggars?

Now there we walk without needing to pick our steps,
Nor shame ourselves to turn a blind eye
Or deaf ear to any wretched soul.

Crossing the wide Pacific and thirty tossing years,
Would you claim a right to comment or criticize?
Should it have ended in an oath sworn this ocean side?
Yet this incense will still burn, and the smoke rise.

12

I wish you the faults calm and rivers tame.
I wish you mild winds and timely rain.
I wish you rich harvest and cattle on wide prairies feed.
I wish you factories hum and fast trains
Whistle and hurtle across the plains.
I wish you from wells from which bountiful oil endlessly flow.
I wish you population slow to grow,
Harmony among citizens, and comity of nations
In centuries of peace so.

L.1976

Fantasia at Christmas Break

1

After yearlong of classroom, lab, and committee maze,
It is time to steal a moment, a duration,
To indulge myself to a pause and gaze.

2

See the clouds beyond the rooftop,
The crimson glow of the setting sun.
Listen to the chirping sparrows under the eaves,
Wings fluttering, collecting the last warm rays of the day.
Winter nights are long.
The meek shall inherit the earth.

3

What is this stirring underneath?
Over layers of complexities,
The complexities of life do us vex.
Only simple death would end them.
Yet it's not upon us to choose.
What child would ponder over the paramount parental gift?
Our Father which art in heaven, hallowed be Thy name.

4

To honor and treasure the gift,
A workaday life should suffice.
One boards the boat on the complex sea
Being loaded by desire, first only from need,
By increments of metamorphosed greed:
Limelight of glory, a pot of gold,
A fiery body, and a lofty rank,
Commander-in-chief or perhaps a Nobel,
Until the overladen vessel foundered and sank--
A tainted House and a painted mouse.[37]
Lead us not into temptation.

5

Inside the ivy-covered building,
An aged full professor ponders his state:
A mere teacher, a bootless rank without a grant.
The young Turks cry out, "Boot the old dud out!"
Another pacing in the corridor would complain.
To anyone who'd listen, no one would fund my plan
To map out a flight to Mars.
Managers of the hall of Socrates counseled,
"Hitch your wagon to a Washington star
Or take the offer of the title of emeritus."

Late in the afternoon, the day is not done.
He begins his homeward shuffle,
A brief case of paper, the shoulders low,
To be examined before hitting the pillow.

---

[37] References to the Watergate scandal and the 1974 research fraud case
by a scientist in Sloan-Kettering Cancer Center of claiming the color
change painted on a mouse was due to a biochemical treatment.

6

I too have it with me,
Like the air I breathe or food I need.
Thanks to the Golden Mean comes to aid.
Excess signals demise; absence signifies.
Regulate, regulate.
Thy will be done.

7

The day is done.
It is the moments of the after-dinner,
Easy chatting with the children--
Their growth making up for the loss of my youth--
    Bittersweet to last.
Smiles of partner's contentment,
A vaseful of peony, a pillow of graying hair,
Cups of chrysanthemum tea to share,
Parents' voices ten thousand miles on a wire,
Su Dong-Po's moonlit dance
Yeat's golden bird in a gyre,
Serenity of Mozart, and sublimity of Beethoven.

Robert's parents: Father, Wen Ke Li;
Mother, Luo Sheng Hua, 1995.

It is the moments of sweeping the snow off the porch,
Surveying the beach grass in the mirror as I brush,
Structural dynamics and finite element,
The field tests done for the tower's columns,[38]
Having the gas tank filled, composing the annual report,
The morning beating an egg, and the evening a glass of port.
Give us our daily bread.

Robert with assistant Bruce Henley on roof of cooling tower.

8

In this moment of peace, gratitude fills my space,
For the laughter around the kitchen table,
The Book, the sages and the bards,
For the old land that formed my being,
For the new that nurtures, magnifying light and space,
For this duration of rest and restoration.

---

[38] Related to a consulting work on the cooling tower of a power plant.

In this pure time, the snake of cynicism finds no entry,
The crows fold their wings and hold their tongue,
The hyenas go hiding,
The layers of complexities are sheared.
Thoughts of love and kindliness of the year
Are sprinkled dews of blessings,
Acts of compassion consecrated.
Lift up your head.
For thine is the kingdom, the power, and the glory.

9

The snowflakes tap the window,
Like the silly moths only a few months ago.
The flickering flames slow their dance on the logs.
I'll go to bed now and maybe have a dreamless sleep.

L.1974

Song of Spring

1

The dark billows churn and turn slow.
In a flash, the sky cracks open in a roar
Into the bare breast of the earth.
The deluge starts to pour.

The young Spring Goddess' tantrum blows over.
The flood recedes. Silver shafts
Thrust from the retreating clouds.
Over the emerald-stippled yard, a robin wafts,
Lands, picks up a writhing worm,
One hop, stares, and flutters past.

The leaves make their appearance,
Greening the hedges by the house edges.
In the breeze, drooping willows
Ripple like the tresses of striding lasses.
The sensuous magnolia, the pure trilliums,
And the crabapple all blossom in their best,
Like vying in a beauty contest.

2

I'd walk among the flowers
And smell their soft petals.
The swaying boughs fondle the nape.
I'd look up and echo to the cardinals,
Tease the fluttering butterflies,
And catch the cottonwood flurries.
I would go and lie down by the creek.
The ripple-riding breeze tucks the hair.
Tender grass brushes the cheek.
Heart beats with the pulsating air.
Blood flows with the wimpling stream.
Notions evolve with the cumuli,
Closing the eyes into a dream.

3

What indulgence!
Who is to sweat in the fields to grow the grain?
Deliver the mail in the rain?
Bear the cacophony of the assembly line?
Pound the roofing nails in sunshine?

4

Graying hair and blurry sight, my spring has left,
The days and years fade away,
Like the withdrawing whistle of a night train.
The field narrows, and options diminish.
Would there be a few more springs that remain?
For this one, nature's work will also soon finish;
Goslings grow to be geese cruising the pond.
Be prepared to account for yours after it's gone.

L.1973

Song of Autumn

1

The sun has begun its decline,
Weakening rays unable to hold the departing geese.
The thought, lost for a moment in the receding vee,
Returns with the squinting eyes.
Russet leaves, tumbling,
Caught in the stubbles of the withering weeds,
And again jerked free by the puffing breeze,
Resume their tumbling, whirl, and reel
Down the fallow mead.

After-school children gather watching
The bumblebees in a daze and half numb
Stumbling among the pale yellow petals
Of the indifferent chrysanthemums.

2

When will the dark curtain fall?
Enveloping the actor in disguise,
Years of disguise –
Has the mask the masker possessed.
A small time peddler, crippled by anxieties,
Chained by vanities, walking a tightrope
Between the seen and unseen,

Clinging to a thread of the soul;
Joints tight, skin sagging from firewood thighs,
Travels and acts, --smiles
Formed from the offset jaw.
Uncertainty of truth stretches the intestines taut.
Arrogance of power powerless to dare,
Rudeness of youth to bear,
Without youth of his own to laugh off the disregard,
Nor wealth to insulate the insult,
Name to forestall the slight,
Or talent to match the pride.
Yet the curtain—

3

Halt! Turn and behold!
The colors! The glorious colors of the woods!
The undulations of gold
By the river bend on the rolling hill!
What splendor and grandeur!
What rhythm and dignity!
A full blast of a magnificent symphony!

Through tender budding in the chill,
Gusty storms, blazing heat, summer hail,
Greedy caterpillars, foul fowls, dirty flies,
Leaves, dried sinews, and scars, all
Have survived and grown to provide
For roots, branches, and fruits alike.
Even the lowly brambles by the dusty road
Proclaim in bright red and yellow hue.
The decorations are their due.

4

The colors will soon fade, and woods grow
Dreary in midst of passionless snow.
Don't let the thought trouble you.
Think of the verdant years,
Of the soft words stroking the ears,
Spoken in the early morning of the spring
In the rose-scented breeze in the summer night.

Think of the tribulations in the ancient land,
The convulsions heralding the rebirth of a giant,
The odysseys, the transplant,
And the struggles and sweat to build a nest
In the erstwhile foreign forest.

Snowy woods

Therefore, hold your cup, not full but fully earned.
Hold it by the crackling wood slowly burned,
A sip for the bitter, a drink of the sweet.
Rest, you will rest this autumn eve.
Mind not the wind is chasing the autumn leaves.
Surely in time the same wind
Will turn mild, heralding a spring.

Thoughts on Christmas Day

1

Christmas is about peace.
The horrors in Indo-China won't cease.
A baby pressed its head to the mother's chest.
The sister squeezed against her thigh.
Three throbbing hearts and six frightened eyes,
Gaping at a smoking barrel held high,
Soon joined the sprawling bodies on the ground.
Hearts cease beating; the unclosed eyes
Stare into the deeps of the blue sky—
Blank but for a solemn eagle
Circling above a village called My Lai.

The scripted act is done before the film crew.
The prisoners returned to muggy dens to brew
Their agony for freedom and home.
Kinfolk by Christmas trees wait in gloom.
Little children ask, "Where is Dad?"
Young mother drowns an eye,
Wetting the single pillow on a double bed.
The well of tears is drained nearly dry.
There's still one-half of the year's longest night.

2

By the Mediterranean and in the Holy Land,
Strands of history and justice snarl;
Blinding passions squeezing the knots,
Out spills Semitic blood darkening the ancient sands
Bearing the footprints of the Prince of Peace
To His birthday we are giving thanks.

3

Christmas is about love.
Below the Equator, the Andes quaked.
A chunk of the mountain dropped into the lake.
A wall of water, rock, and mud
Thundered down the valley,
Crushing the homespun Indian huts
And gulping alive the city of Yunggay,
Whose petrified dwellers are to be dug
Out as objects of curiosity
And inquiry, like those of Pompeii,
By students of archaeology
In a mutated generation of another age.

4

The big wind whirled on the coast of Bangladesh,
Conjuring the wrath of the deep water
Of the Bengal Bay, working a monstrous wash.

Days after the fury and rage were spent,
Numbed survivors stumbled in the stench
Among the crops and corpses

Rotting under the sun, blazing and blank
In three hundred thousand tolls for the souls,
Lost in a single sweep of nature's hand!

5

Nature ordains its creatures to strive
To survive, dominate, and spread.
Men follow but can't do them without greed,
Bringing struggles, wars, and bloodshed.
Even in a world of democracies,
Saints and sages do not have enough votes
To alter the fate to which nature would seem to lead.

Perhaps the dread of a universal death
Of the instant or lingering kind, bearing this year
The Nonproliferation Treaty of Nuclear Weapons
And the Celebration Earth Day,
Could work a reversal of our fate.

Now for what profit it is for a mere academic
To take it upon himself to ponder over
The miseries, injustices, and pain of the world,
Living with the mysteries of God's nature and its
        subset man?
You can do no better than to work to mitigate them
And find the comfort and joy the best you can.

An organism thus far safely alive,
I ought to just thank my new roots and clime,
Where I can freely think and write

To soothe the conscience of a limited mind.
I will celebrate this Christmas Day
By getting on my knees and bowing my head.
Thy kingdom come! Thy will be done!

Part 4
Chinese Poems

立秋

酣眠乍醒夢難訴;
風陣雨急秋勁奏.
輾轉尋睡擾褥床;
一揮纏被上書房.

西川遊

1

任說年老蜀道難，
還是去吧狂一狂！
三千里更太平洋，
西藏飯店綉花床。
顛簸盡日車內歌，
車外*唱歌*不可擋[39]。

晚間小爐保溫馨，
清晨來到珍珠灘。
湍流飛瀑天上景，
松嶂碧池神仙境。
夜曲顫喉[40]抖心絃；
白絲披肩增客興。

2

四千米上岷江碑，
舉臂嘯呼犛背座。
古鎮松潘雨如絲，
麻婆豆腐紅發紫。

---

[39] 導遊用"唱歌"作"方便"的代詞。
[40] 戲院藏族表演。

3

汶州茶館待路通：
四川麻將只許*碰*[41]；
一杯菊花枸杞子，
聆聽佛諦增慧智。
倚壁山路懼崢嶸；
暮色迷蒙到臥龍。

4

七十熊貓千百片；
攀臥嚼竹皆愛遍。
汝等不如少繁殖；
爲數過多日來賤。

一州魚咀分二江；
二道再分流四鄉。
如此沃肥大成都；
滔滔江水千年糧。

5

金沙遺址懷前先；
世级博宫今日羨。
雅安路旁小酒店，
斧落鰱首遊客宴。

環繞瀘定萬重山，
左右上下十百遍。
康定情歌大酒店，
亞歷山大波斯軍，

---

[41] 不許 "吃"。(Only "three of a kind" type of form [*peng*] is allowed to incorporate a discarded block.)

流遷混遺帥哥種，
遠道女客看不厭。

6

大度河上浪濤濤；
兩岸通靠鉄索橋。
日煦風急竟搖晃，
嬌女緊抓不敢瞧。

7

磨西明珠大酒店，
房樓幢幢皆幽雅；
晚餐電停看不見。
晨曦映峰金燦爛；
十天徒步徒携傘。

索道車廂瞰冰景，
冰河兩側聳雪山。
三號營地雪與冰，
青稞餅沾犛肉湯，
寒風侵衣熱手心。
泉水氤氳池上池，
四方秀女羞哧哧。

坦胸勇士將拍照，
笑語盈盈下水遲。

8

二郎隧道四千米；
樂山大佛船上禮。
磁热宴畢去峨嵋；
四星酒店洗塵灰。

9

旅車兜上峨嵋山；
云翳繚繞梵樂漫。
傍午霧散方見佛，
路陡石滑逞雄不。
覩朓休省滑竿錢；
來到山底骨肉全。

10

旬日不問凡塵事，
课堂经费患得失。
身憊心悦歸蘭馨；
熙熙攘攘再一世。
儘他腊月凜冽冬；
閉眼盡回心目中。

時事

煞斯[42]惡病前不知，
口罩警心思禦之。
伊[43]众號啕痛火爐，
阿拉[44]何苦賜油池。

---

[42] SARS 流行病。
[43] 伊拉克。
[44] Allah（上帝）。

悦山美地[45](Yosemite)

洲盤抗轧萬千年。
徐舉花崗蔽半天。
凍涧磨山冰化漫。
泉流土礫谷中填。

循環日月生亡代。
拜日红杉直擎天。
早主耶穌七百載。
悦山美地聖風甜。

蓝绒閃爍鑽嵌天。
木舍黄燈小路邊。
细语家常爐氣暖。
風停夜静自成眠。

---

[45] 1993 年十月，長子文堅邀其父母遊覽加州景区Yosemite三日。身疲神
怡。作文以誌此樂事。Yosemite 發音好似 "悦山美地。"

白崖點绿百年松。
石壓狂根虎鬧龍。
豺嘯獐奔松鼠躍。
银溪濺壁掛穹虹。

兒攙母手徐徐上。
父背影機喘喘登。
乍诧今生行啥善。
悦山美地享天倫。

黑裘衣⁴⁶

年少無力華衣购; 愛出風頭。
　愛出風頭。
父親西服伴女友。

如今粉筆換黑裘, 豈管面皺。
　豈管面皺。
强挺疲背摇摇走。

---

⁴⁶ 1991 年二月, 一州末去Ann Arbor 訪友, 吃點心, 身穿黑皮夹克。友
笑言:"好顯年轻噢!" 我以上作答; 大家開開心。

C.1973 (S)

冬末

白雪輕蓋地；
裊裊上炊煙。
變幻蓝雲慢；
人思宇宙邊。

C.1970 (S.2)

送行

少年將上路。
愛母给私金。
女子偷流淚。
嚴亲警小心。

Printed in the United States
By Bookmasters